73 -

# PLAY CHESS

# Play Chess

**WILLIAM HARTSTON & JEREMY JAMES**

BRITISH BROADCASTING CORPORATION

Published by the
British Broadcasting Corporation
35 Marylebone High Street
London W1M 4AA

ISBN 0 563 17881 7
First published 1980
© William Hartston & Jeremy James 1980

Printed in England
by Jolly & Barber Ltd, Rugby

# Foreword

When I was six I thought all chess players were very, very old, smoked pipes, and *never* smiled. And in those days perhaps chess was an old man's game.

Nowadays however chess belongs to children of all ages, and some of the top chess players in the world are quite young. Anatoly Karpov, the reigning World Champion, is twenty-nine and was only eighteen when he became an International Master and nineteen when he became a Grandmaster.

Here in Britain, chess is very much the young person's game. More and more boys and girls are playing chess in schools and clubs, as well as at home. One day perhaps one of our young players will be World Champion. Britain's first Grandmaster was Tony Miles (at one time the world's youngest Grandmaster), and fifteen-year-old International Master Nigel Short has already been tipped as a future World Champion.

Bill Hartston, co-author of this book, and chess commentator for BBC2's *Master Game* and BBC1's *Play Chess*, is another of Britain's young chess players. He won the London under-sixteen championship in 1962, became an International Master in 1972 (when he was twenty-five), was British Champion in 1973 and 1975 and won the BBC Master Game Trophy in 1975 and 1976. In *Play Chess* Bill Hartston and Jeremy James describe the basic rules of the game, but also introduce the young player to some of the tricks and stratagems that make chess such an exciting game.

I think their aim is to make sure that all chess players are very, very young, suck lollipops and always *always* smile.

I wish I were six again!

*Mark Patterson*
Producer, *Play Chess*

| The pieces | Symbols | Abbreviations |
|---|:---:|:---:|
| The White King | | *K* |
| The White Queen | | *Q* |
| A White Rook | | *R* |
| A White Bishop | | *B* |
| A White Knight | | *N* |
| A White Pawn | | ° |
| | | |
| The Black King | | *K* |
| The Black Queen | | *Q* |
| A Black Rook | | *R* |
| A Black Bishop | | *B* |
| A Black Knight | | *N* |
| A Black Pawn | | ° |

° Pawns do not have an abbreviation in the text – if no letter precedes the move that indicates that the piece moved is a pawn.

# ONE: Introduction

Chess is one of the oldest and best wargames in the world, not that it is quite as violent as it has been in the past. Players do not hit each other with the board or hurl pieces at their opponents with quite the abandon that once seemed almost normal. It is rather more elegant than that, a war between two courts as it were.

There stands the King, with his advisor the Queen on his left. There are the two ministers, the Bishops, ready to go off on their slippery missions; at their sides, those tricky envoys the Knights, who can leap to places no other piece can reach; and there on the edge of the board, those fortress-like pieces which look like castles but are called Rooks glower threateningly at each other.

In front of these powerful pieces are the footsoldiers, the infantry of the game, the Pawns. The Duke of Wellington once said that every private carried a field-marshal's baton in his haversack, by which he meant anyone with drive and ambition could reach the very top, and so it is with the pawn as you will see. If it can survive the canon and musketry of the game and get the whole length of the board, then it too can reach the very top and become that strongest piece, the Queen.

So, at the beginning of the game, each player has sixteen pieces at his command; one King, one Queen, two Rooks, two Bishops, two Knights and eight Pawns. And to make it easy to follow in diagrams, each piece has a symbol, as shown opposite.

So there are two courts arrayed for battle. Now, what are you going to try to do? Each side is going to try to attack and capture the opposing King. Nothing could be easier, could it? Except that while you're trying to attack your opponent, he is trying to do the same to you, so you have to think about defending your King as well as attacking your opponent.

To do this, the pieces each have moves of their own: Pawn, Knight, Bishop, Rook, Queen and King.

This is what the board looks like before you start.

Notice that the Queen always starts on her own colour, and there is a white square in the right-hand corner of the board when you sit down. Get that wrong, and the whole game becomes chaos.

Some pieces are much stronger than others and are therefore much more valuable. An easy way of remembering that is to give the pieces points according to their value. A Queen is worth nine points, the Rooks are worth five points each, the Bishops and Knights are all worth three points, and the Pawns are worth a point apiece. The King is so important he does not have a value. If you lose him, you lose the game. As you can see, all the strong pieces are hiding behind the Pawns at the start of the game. So let's take everything off the board and see just what they can all do.

Even though he starts the game apparently tucked away out of the action on the very corner of the board, the Rook is immensely strong. As long as there is nothing in the way, he can move as far as he likes up and down the board (up and down what are called 'files') or across the board (the rows of squares across the board are called 'ranks'). What he cannot do is change direction in the middle of a move. If there is a piece in the way, he either has to stop or, if it is an enemy piece, he can take it. When you take in chess, you end up with your piece on the square that was occupied by the piece you've taken; you do not jump over it. The arrows show all the moves a Rook can make.

The Bishop is almost the same, except he moves along what are called diagonals. He takes in exactly the same way as the Rook. As you can see, a Bishop stays on the same coloured squares as the colour of the square where he began the game. For instance, White's King's Bishop starts on a white square and always moves on white squares.

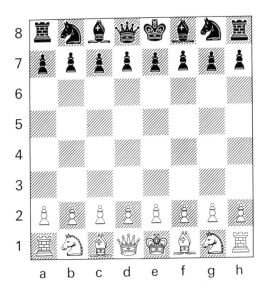

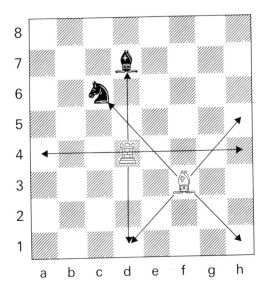

The Queen is the most powerful single piece on the board. On her move, she can either go up and down the files or along the ranks like a Rook, or along the diagonals like a Bishop. In one move, she can only do one or the other; she cannot start like a Rook, then suddenly change direction and go on like a Bishop.

The Knight is a very tricky little piece. His moves look complicated, but they are not really as difficult as they seem. He goes two squares forward, then one sideways; or one square forward and then two sideways; or two backwards, then one sideways; or one backwards and two sideways. He is also the only piece on the board that can jump over another.

The King moves exactly like the Queen, except that he can only move one square in any direction at a time. When he is attacked by a piece, he is in what is called 'check'. On the left-hand side of the diagram opposite, the Black King is being attacked by the White Rook. Now, he has three ways of getting out of check. He can either move to one of the squares shown – but not the other one next to him because he would still be in check – or the Knight can take the Rook, or the Knight can go between the King and Rook.

On the right-hand side of the diagram opposite, the Black King is in check again from a White Rook. But this time, whichever square he moves to he is still in check from one or other of the White Rooks. The Black Knight can neither take the Rook attacking the King nor get between the King and Rook. That is what is called 'checkmate'. To preserve the King's dignity, White does not take the King off the board; he just says 'checkmate' – preferably without gloating – and the game is over.

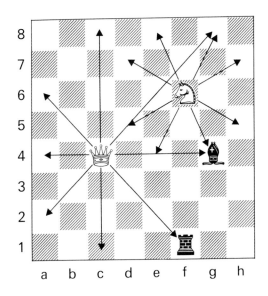

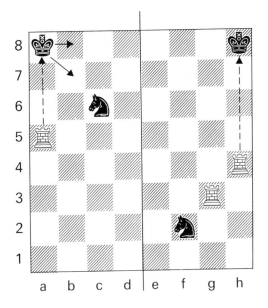

The King and the Rook have a rather complicated-looking but very vital combined move. Once in a game, they have the privilege of moving together. The King moves two squares towards the Rook which jumps over him to finish on the square next to the King. It is called castling. In the diagram, the White King could castle but has not; the Black King, which was in the same position as the White King, has castled.

Castling is only allowed if: first, there are no pieces between the King and Rook; second, neither the King nor Rook has moved previously; third, the King is not in check; fourth, the King does not move into check or over a square where he would be in check if he stopped. So, in the diagram, the White King can castle on the King's side but not on the Queen's side because he would be in check from the Black Bishop on the square where he ended.

So, last but not least, to the not so humble Pawn. A Pawn moves straight down the board one square at a time, with two exceptions. On its first move, a Pawn can go forward two squares. That is what the Pawn in front of the White King has done. Also, if it wants to take, it does not take any piece directly in front of it; it takes a piece diagonally in front. For instance, White's 'b' Pawn can take either the Pawn or the Knight diagonally in front.

If a Pawn gets right down the board to the eighth rank, it is instantly promoted – usually to a Queen, she being the strongest piece, or to any piece you choose except a King.

Remember that in Chess, unlike Draughts, you don't have to take your opponent's pieces, but if you think you can gain an advantage by doing so, then do. And also remember, when you do take you put your piece on the square that was occupied by the piece you have taken. You do not jump over.

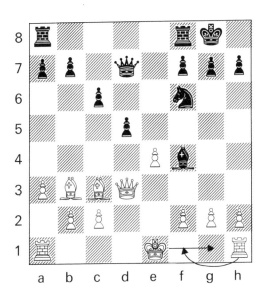

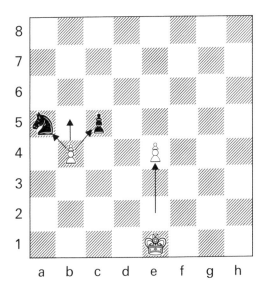

As you read this book and then go on to read other books and watch television programmes about Chess, you will see that there are various ways of describing moves and recording games. The most common is called 'algebraic' and is the one we'll use in this book. The other most common systems are described in the last chapter along with all sorts of other useful bits and pieces of information.

If you look at the diagram opposite, you'll see there are eight files – that is, lines of squares going up and down the board. Starting from the left, they are given letters from 'a' to 'h'. At the same time, the ranks – the lines of squares going across the board, are numbered from 1 to 8. In diagrams, the White pieces are always at the bottom of the board, the Black pieces at the top. So, for instance, the White King always starts on e1 and the Black King on e8. If you want to move the White King to f2, you simply write down Ke1–f2. If he takes, you put an 'x' (Ke1xf2); when a check is given, + is written after the move.

Now is the time to practise what all the pieces can do and record what they have done. It is easier if you set up a board and then play the following few moves to see exactly how the system works. K = King, Q = Queen, R = Rook, B = Bishop, N = Knight (not K because it would be confused with the King). For Pawn moves, you do not bother to write 'P' each time. You simply put the square it started from and the square it ended. Castling is written 0–0 on the King's side and 0–0–0 on the Queen's side. White always starts, so the White moves are in the left-hand columns and the Black moves in the right-hand columns.

| 1 | e2–e4 | e7–e5 | 5 | Nb1–c3 | Bf8–b4 |
|---|--------|--------|---|---------|--------|
| 2 | Ng1–f3 | Nb8–c6 | 6 | Nd4xc6 | d7xc6 |
| 3 | d2–d4 | e5xd4 | 7 | Bf1–d3 | 0–0 |
| 4 | Nf3xd4 | Ng8–f6 | | | |

Just one final point of notation: you'll sometimes see ! or ? written after a move. An exclamation mark means a good move, while ? means a bad move. Especially good or bad moves earn !! or ??

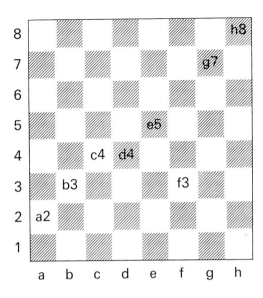

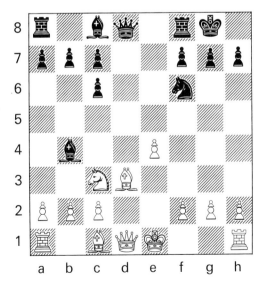

White has just played his Rook to
h3 checking the King on h8. Has
Black lost, or can he find a square
where he is not in check?

White has played his Rook to d8,
check. Is Black checkmate or not?
Don't forget the way a Knight
moves.

In this position, the White King
has obviously been on a very long
tour of the board. He has just
moved from f6 to f7. Is that the
end of his journey or can Black
leap free?

White has just played his Queen
to h4 mate! Or is it?

You'll find the answers to all
these puzzles at the back, starting
on page 92.

# TWO: The Pieces

Quite why a Rook should be called a Rook is one of life's little mysteries. In the earliest days of chess, the Rook was a chariot. Then during the Crusades, when everyone was building castles to defend themselves against attack, it became a Castle. In some languages it still is called a Castle: in French, for instance, it is 'la Tour' and in German 'der Turm'. Just to be completely different, in Russian it is a boat!

Ever since the very earliest days of chess, the moves a Rook can make have been the same. It has always been able to go as far as there is room in straight lines along the ranks and files. As you can see, if you set the pieces up, there is not much a Rook can do early in the game. He is all boxed in by his own pieces. But as the game goes on and pawns and other pieces are exchanged, so there are wider spaces for the Rook's operations. So do not be in too much of a hurry to use Rooks in the early stages of the game.

Apart from the Queen, he is the most powerful piece on the board and worth keeping in reserve until there are enough lines open for him to operate effectively. When he does have space, he is a ferocious attacking piece because he is not slow-moving like the Knight and is not for ever stuck on squares of one colour like the Bishop.

A Rook is worth about half the value of the Queen, but is worth about two pawns more than a Knight or Bishop – or almost twice as much. He is so strong that just one Rook, helped by his King, can checkmate the enemy King.

When you have a Rook on the board, always look out for possibilities to attack two of your opponent's pieces on the same line. You would be surprised how often players can leave their King and Queen in line with one another, and give you the chance to win the Queen for a Rook. Set up the position shown in the diagram on your own board. You'll see that the Black King and Queen are both on the same rank, and that gives White just the chance his Rook needs. By playing 1 Ra7–a5 White will win the Queen for his Rook. Why is this so? Well, the Rook on a5 attacks the Queen and threatens to take her next move, and she can't escape! If she tries to run out of the way up or down the board she will leave her own King in check from the Rook, and that she is not allowed to do. She can run sideways, staying between Rook and King, but she will not be able to escape from the Rook's attack. So Black has nothing better than to take the terrible Rook with the Queen when she is immediately captured herself by the White King. White wins Queen for Rook, a very big gain for him.

This was an example of the *pin*, one of the most important attacking ideas in chess. Usually when you attack one of your opponent's pieces he just moves it away (if he sees that you are attacking it, of course). What's much better is to attack something which can't move away, like the poor Queen we just looked at. If you attack a piece which can't move away because there's something even more important behind it, that is called a pin. Imagine a long pin coming from the White Rook on a5, sticking all the way through the Queen and pinning her to the King, and you'll see why this kind of attack is called a pin. You'll also understand how uncomfortable the poor Queen feels to be pinned by the Rook. So when your Rooks can move to open files (up and down the board) or ranks (across the board) to attack your opponent's pieces, remember to look behind those pieces as well. If something big is hiding behind, the pin can win!

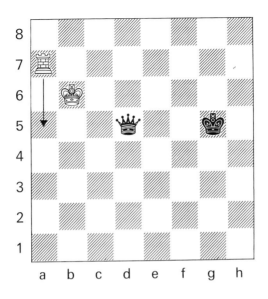

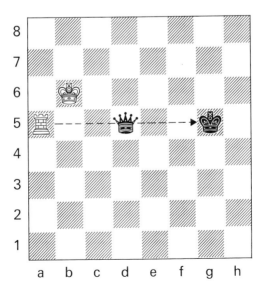

But the pin isn't the only way a Rook can win material. There is another attacking idea which is just as nasty. Let's go back to the first position on page 19, but this time pretend that it's Black's move. He sees that White wants to pin the Queen by moving his Rook to a5, so he might decide that it's time to move the Queen off the dangerous fifth rank. So Black plays 1 . . ., Qd5–g2??

Remember two question marks means a really horrible blunder. Now what's so horrible? The Queen has after all moved off the dangerous square. Yes, that's true, but she has moved on to an even worse one. Now Queen and King are again on the same line – the g-file. White plays 2 Ra7–g7+ saying 'check' to the Black King. Just look at the position. The Black King must move out of check, but then his Queen will be exposed to the White Rook's attack. The Rook will take the Queen and Black loses a whole Queen.

This type of attack, which is very similar to the pin, is called an X-Ray attack. The Rook in the diagram attacks the Queen by X-Ray through the King. Some people call it a skewer and say that the Queen is skewered by the Rook. That sounds even more painful.

There's one more idea using the Rook which is even stronger than the pin or the X-Ray attack. Those are fine ways to win pieces, but this one can finish the game at once. Look at the position in the diagram. The Black King looks nice and safe behind its cosy defensive wall of pawns, but White to move plays 1 Rb1–b8! and suddenly the game is over. It is checkmate. The Rook covers the whole of the back rank to stop the King moving sideways, while Black's own pawns prevent the King from going forward. Unfortunately, the rules do not let Black capture his own pieces so the King is trapped. This is called a Back Rank Mate and has been the sudden finish to thousands of chess games. When you have castled, and think your King is safely tucked away, look out for those Back Rank Mates – they can be fatal!

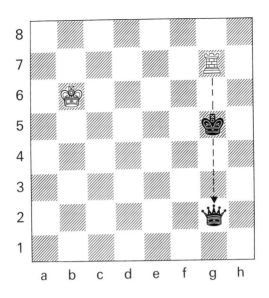

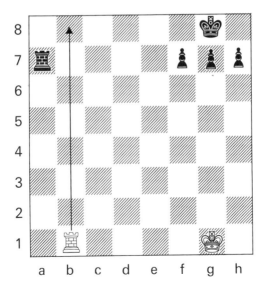

## The Rook – Puzzles

PUZZLE 1.

White to move, how can he win one of the Black Rooks?

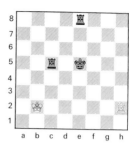

PUZZLE 2.

White to play. Can he give checkmate?

PUZZLE 3.

The White Bishop on d2 is pinned to the Rook on d1.
Can you see what White can do to turn the tables?

PUZZLE 4.

Black to move this time. Should he capture the Pawn on e6 with his King, or with his Queen?

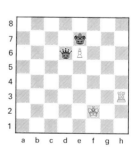

22

## 2 The Knight

The Knight is another piece whose moves have not changed since the very earliest days of chess. In *Through the Looking Glass* the White Knight was a most curious character, carrying not only a spear and sword but such unwarlike objects as saucepans, and he was always falling off. Perhaps the man who wrote about him, Lewis Carroll, was not a very good chess player and did not really understand what a Knight could do.

The Knight certainly is a strange piece. He is the only piece not to move in straight lines (although if you ask any Knight how he moves, he will insist that he does move straight to his chosen square).

He is worth about the same as a Bishop, but has a totally different and more devious character. No Bishop can ever hope to see more than half the squares on the board – all those of the same colour as the one he started from – but a Knight can reach every single one of them.

There is one very important advantage the Knight has. He can jump over other pieces. When none of the other pieces can operate properly because all their lines are blocked by Pawns or other pieces, the Knight is truly happy because he can just hop over whatever might be in his way.

Never forget that your Knights are happiest in the middle of the board. Put a Knight on the board and then see if you can count how many squares he can reach from where you put him. If you put him in the corner, you will see that he can only go to two different squares. He is not very much better off on the edge of the board, with no more than three or four possible moves. But put him in the wide open spaces of the middle of the board, and you will see that he has no less than eight moves to choose from. His effect can be felt all over the board and he does not seem such a slow piece after all. In fact he is very dangerous because it is so easy to overlook what he is attacking; so, beware the enemy Knight that approaches your King.

When we talked about the Rook, we met the pin and the X-Ray, two ways of attacking pieces which cannot run away. Another easy way is to attack two of them at the same time, something which the Knight can do especially well. When you attack two pieces at the same time, it is called a Fork, and the Knight Fork is the most common fork of all. The real reason why the Knight can be such an amazing nuisance is that he can attack anything (except another Knight) without any danger of being captured by the piece he attacks. Even a Queen must run away from a Knight which is attacking her. Look at the position shown in the diagram: the White Knight attacks King and Queen at the same time. When the King moves out of check, as he must, the Knight will capture the Queen. Knight forks can happen anywhere on the board. You should try on your own board, putting the Black King on e5, as in the diagram, then putting the Black Queen on another black square. See if you can find a square where a White Knight can fork King and Queen. For instance, with the Queen on h8, White can fork with a Knight on g6 or f7. If the Queen is on g1 a Knight on f3 does the trick. In fact there are only five safe black squares on the board for the Queen where she cannot be forked by a Knight. See if you can find all of them.

There is another trick with the Knight which is even more deadly than the fork. This is called the Smothered Mate. Set up the starting position for a new game and play the moves.

1   e2–e4    c7–c6
2   d2–d4    d7–d5
3   Nb1–c3   d5xe4
4   Nc3xe4   Nb8–d7
5   Qd1–e2   Ng8–f6?? (see the diagram)

And now White played 6 Ne4–d6 and the game was over. Black's King is in check from the Knight and is completely hemmed in by his own pieces. He can't even take the Knight because, although it looks as though his e-pawn is attacking it, 6 . . . e7xd6 would open the e-file and expose the King to check from the White Queen on e2. So Black is checkmated, smothered to death by his own pieces. That was one of the shortest games ever played in an international tournament.

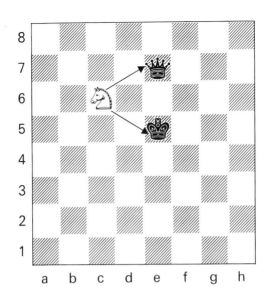

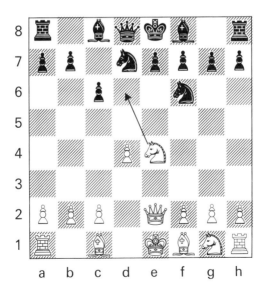

Here's another example of how a smothered mate can happen. This time it's not just the result of a blunder; Black wins by a brilliant attacking idea. From the position shown opposite, he forces checkmate in five moves, despite the fact that White has more pieces.

Black starts with 1 . . . Qe7–e3+ and the White King must move out of check. If he goes to f1, then the Black Queen will come and sit next to him on f2, defended by the Knight, and say 'checkmate' (we'll talk more about this sort of checkmate when we come to the section about the Queen). So White plays 2 Kg1–h1. Now the Knight comes in with a check: 2 . . . Ng4–f2+ and White must go back again with 3 Kh1–g1. Black checks again: 3 . . . Nf2–h3+! Look at this, it's a double check! White's King is attacked by both Queen and Knight. White cannot take the Knight with his pawn on g2, because he would still be in check from the Queen. So he must play 4 Kg1–h1 again. And now comes the beautiful point: 4 . . . Qe3–g1+!! But what's this? Black is putting his queen on a square where it can be taken. 5 Rc1xg1 (White cannot take with the King, since he would then be in check from the Knight at h3). And now do you see the point of Black's play? White's King is surrounded by its own men: 5 . . . Nh3–f2 and the wonder horse has triumphed again. (*See diagram position.*) The White King is checkmate, once again suffocated by its own men and killed by a Knight.

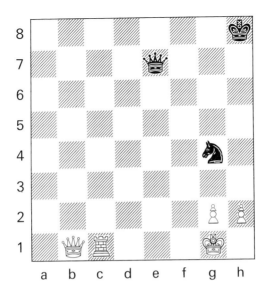

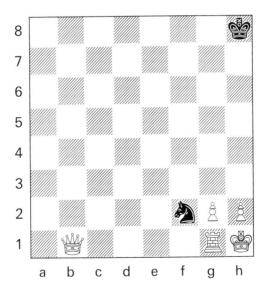

## The Knight – Puzzles

PUZZLE 1.

White to play. Spot the Knight fork!

PUZZLE 2.

Not quite the same as the first position. If only the Black King were on h8, the Knight could fork. So what does White play?

PUZZLE 3.

Can you see a way to set up the Black King and Queen for a Knight fork?

PUZZLE 4.

The Black King is out of range of the Knight at the moment. But White can force it closer and the Knight comes in for the kill. How?

## 3 The Bishop

When chess first began, the Bishop was the King's advisor and was nothing like as strong as he is now. He had a most odd move, jumping one square diagonally. In those earliest times he was an elephant, but then as the game developed and the pieces became more abstract, so both his move and his name changed. The slit in the top was meant to represent the lines on an elephant's forehead, but the French thought it was a court jester's hat, so they called him 'le fou' – the fool. The English thought it looked like a Bishop's hat, so they called it a Bishop, while in Germany, because it runs down the diagonals, they called it 'Der Läufer' the runner.

About 400 years ago, they decided chess was too slow and needed speeding up a bit, so they changed the Bishop's move from his quaint little hop to his modern move. Like the Rook, he moves in straight lines, but his lines are the diagonals. He can do almost anything a Rook can do, but his great drawback is that he can only ever move on squares of one colour. You might wonder why a chess board is divided into black and white squares instead of simply having them all one colour; the answer is that it is just to help the Bishops find their way round more easily.

You start the game with two Bishops, one black-squared and one white-squared. Between them, they can cover the whole board, but once you have lost or exchanged one of them, you must take special care of the other and give him all the help you can. If your only Bishop is the white-squared one, for instance, then it is a very good idea to put your pawns on black squares if you can, so that they do not get in the way of the Bishop. And, of course, the other way round if you have a black-squared Bishop. The point is to keep your pieces working happily without getting in each other's way.

Just as the Rook can pin and X-ray on files and ranks, the Bishop can do exactly the same along its own lines of action – the diagonals. Whenever two pieces stand on the same diagonal, they must watch out for a Bishop coming along to attack them. The first diagram is an example of how effective the Bishop pin can be. Black's King and Rook are on the same diagonal from d8 to h4. The White Bishop promptly places itself on that same diagonal at g5: 1 *Bc1–g5!* attacking the Rook and pinning it to the King. The Rook cannot move away without exposing the King to check from the Bishop. Black replies with 1 . . . *Kd8–e7*. Now if White takes Rook with Bishop, Black will recapture Bishop with King, but White has a better opportunity. The Rook is still pinned on the diagonal, so there is time for 2 *e4–e5!* attacking the Rook again. It cannot escape, so next move White will be able to play 3 *e5xf6* winning a whole Rook, not just Rook for Bishop. This shows us an important principle: when you have pinned an enemy piece, try to attack it with as much as possible to ensure that you win something. If it can't move away, why not take advantage of it? In chess, you *do* kick pieces which cannot fight back.

This diagram shows an example of the Bishop's X-Ray attack. Just as the Rook did, the Bishop can check a King and win something big, in this case a Queen which thought it was safely hiding behind the King. Wherever Black moves his King out of check, White will answer by capturing Queen with Bishop.

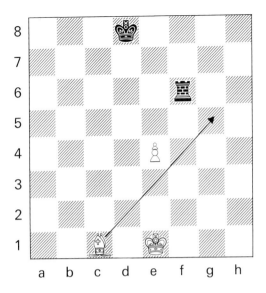

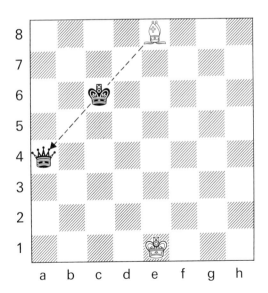

Now here's a much more complicated example of the power of a pin. This is an extraordinary position, showing that thanks to a pin a Bishop can sometimes draw against two Rooks. In the position of the diagram White plays 1 Bd1–f3 pinning the Rook on e4 to the King. Now look at Black's possibilities after this move. He can't move the Rook on e4; if he moves his King, White plays Bf3xe4, winning a whole Rook and reaching a position in which Black cannot win (though Rook is better than Bishop, it cannot win with no other pieces on the board); so he must move the Rook on e5. Moving it along the rank (to f5, g5 or h5) again loses a whole Rook to 2 Bf3xe4+, so Black must move his Rook backwards, say to e8. Now comes the point: after these moves 1 Bd1–f3 Re5–e8, White does not take the pinned Rook. In fact 2 Bf3xe4+ Re8xe4 would win for Black. Instead White just plays 2 Bf3–g2 maintaining the pin. Again Black has nothing to do but move his Rook up the e-file, since King moves again lose a whole Rook. So 2 . . . Re8–e7, for instance, but after 3 Bg2–f3! White still waits and Black can do nothing but go back and forth. The game is a draw. Nobody can win.

One more piece of Bishop virtuosity to end this section. Here we've let a Knight get in on the act. In this position the Black King and Queen are on the same diagonal, so we must think about a pin or skewer from the Bishop, but the naturally attractive move 1 Bf1–b5 does not look so good. Surely Black can just take it with his Queen? The Bishop is not protected on b5. But it is! It's protected by the Knight's magical forking ability. Play goes 1 Bf1–b5! Qc6xb5 2 Nd5–c7+! Black must move his King out of check leaving White to play 3 Nc7xb5. The power of the Bishop pin was just what was needed here to set up a fork for the Knight. A nice example of these two basic attacking ideas working together.

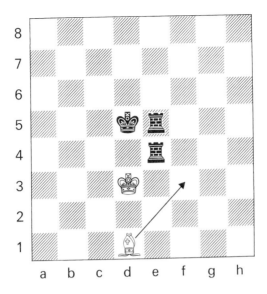

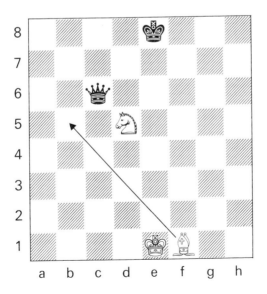

## The Bishop – Puzzles

PUZZLE 1.

How can White lure the Black
King and Queen on to the same
diagonal so that the Bishop can
do its job?

PUZZLE 2.

It's unusual for a Bishop to
checkmate on its own, but often
with the help of another piece
the Bishop will play an
important part in a checkmate.
How does the White Bishop now
set up a threat of mate which
cannot be stopped?

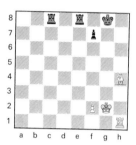

PUZZLE 3.

Bishop and Knight can also work
well together. How do they
combine to give a two-move
checkmate in this position?

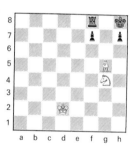

PUZZLE 4.

All the White Bishop on b5 does
is to pin the Pawn on d7. How
did White use this pin to win the
Black Queen in one move?

## 4 The Queen

The Queen is by far the strongest piece on the board. She is worth almost two Rooks, or both Bishops and a Knight, because she can move as far as she likes in any direction she likes, either along the ranks and files or along the diagonals. It used not to be so. She used to be the weakest piece on the board and at one time could only move one square diagonally at a time. There was a brief time in Russia when she was even stronger than she is now because, as well as being able to move like a Rook or Bishop, she could also suddenly slip in a surreptitious Knight's move! Even without that, though, she is the strongest attacking piece on the board.

Curiously, because she does have such an important part to play in attacks, she is vulnerable to attack herself. She is worth so much more than any other piece that you will not want to exchange her for anything else except your opponent's Queen. In the same way as you say 'check' when you attack your opponent's King, so there was a time when you used to warn your opponent when you were attacking his Queen by saying 'gardez la reine'. You don't have to, but it is polite because, if you make a ghastly mistake you do not see and lose your Queen as a result, you have virtually lost the game.

So if your Queen is attacked, you will have to move her away. This means you should think very hard before rushing your Queen into an early attack. What usually happens is that at first your opponent will just defend and will quietly go on mobilising his pieces. Then suddenly he will attack your Queen and you will find her being chased all over the board, lucky even to be able to get her to the safety of home again. Bringing your Queen out too early can give your opponent two targets to attack, your King and your Queen, and it can be most un-comfortable trying to defend both.

Remember your Queen is your strongest piece – treat her with care. Because the Queen is so strong, nearly all games which end in a quick and surprising finish have her to thank (or to blame, if you lose) for the final move. If you play really badly it's actually possible to lose in two moves by letting the opponent's Queen come in to checkmate. This game goes 1 f2–f3 e7–e5 2 g2–g4 Qd8–h4 checkmate (*see diagram*). Look how the White Pawn moves open that diagonal leading to his King. Using just his Queen Black has taken advantage of White's bad moves to give an immediate checkmate. This is called 'Fool's Mate' because you really have to be very foolish to play so badly that you lose in two moves.

There's another famous quick game which ends in checkmate by the Queen, but this one is much more clever and it lasts four moves. It's called 'Scholar's Mate' because, even though the loser still has to be quite foolish and helpful, the winner's ideas are a little more scholarly than in the Fool's Mate which we saw above.

In Scholar's Mate, White starts like this:

1 e2–e4    e7–e5
2 Bf1–c4   Bf8–c5
3 Qd1–h5

Now do you see what the White Queen wants to do? Look along the straight lines leading from her new square. You'll see that she is attacking the Pawn on e5, but she is also attacking something more important. Sometimes Black only sees this first attack and decides to defend the e-Pawn with 3 . . . Nb8–c6?? And now comes the sudden end:

4 Qh5xf7 checkmate!

That's the position in the diagram – Scholar's Mate. The Queen on f7 is defended by the Bishop on c4. Black's King is in check and has nowhere to run. The game is over. Of course what Black should have done on his third move was to see both White's attacks and defend both of them with 3 . . . Qd8–e7. That protects both Pawns on e5 and f7, so White cannot take either without losing a piece.

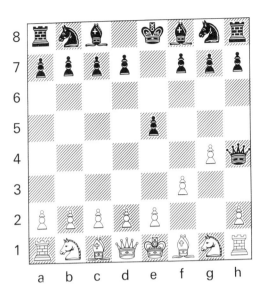

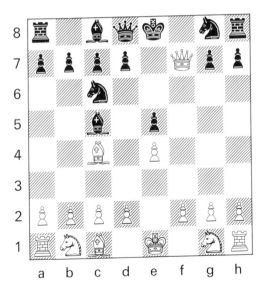

Scholar's Mate tells us something else very important about the Queen. You can see from the final position just how dangerous it is to let your opponent's Queen sit next to your King. The Queen is so strong that she can cover all the squares round a King which is sitting at the edge of the board. We have seen that a Rook or Knight can win a game on their own, but they really need quite a lot of help from the opponent's pieces getting in the way of their own King. The Queen can give checkmate much more easily, with very little help at all. Set up the position opposite on your own board. White has only a Pawn near the Black King, but he can force checkmate by bringing his Queen to attack. After 1 Qc1–h6 White threatens 2 Qh6–g7 mate. And there is nothing Black can do about it. His King cannot run away (1 . . . Kg8–f8 is not possible and 1 . . . Kg8–h8 does not help since 2 Qh6–g7 is still mate). None of the Black pieces can prevent the Queen coming to g7, so next move the game will be over.

Of course, the Queen is good at many other things too, besides giving checkmates. She moves like a Rook and a Bishop, so she can perform all the Pins and Skewers or X-Ray attacks that those pieces can do. But the Queen also has her own special ability to fork – attacking two unprotected pieces at the same time. Especially dangerous are those forks where she attacks one piece like a Rook and another like a Bishop. A player once lost a game in four moves in an international team tournament because he overlooked such a fork. The game went like this:

$$1 \; e2–e4 \qquad c7–c5$$
$$2 \; d2–d4 \qquad c5xd4$$
$$3 \; Ng1–f3 \qquad e7–e5$$
$$4 \; Nf3xe5?$$

and now Black played 4 . . . Qd8–a5+ (*see diagram*). The Queen gives check like a bishop and attacks the Knight like a Rook. The Knight is lost.

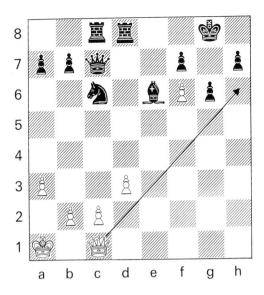

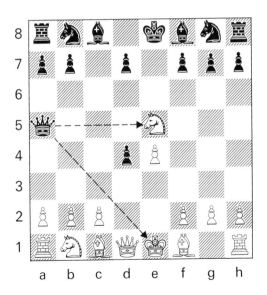

## The Queen – Puzzles

PUZZLE 1.

White's Queen can give check in seven ways in this position, but one of them is checkmate. Which one?

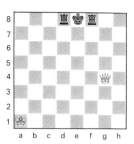

PUZZLE 2.

White's Bishop on d3 is pinned to his Queen by the Black Queen. What should White do about it?

PUZZLE 3.

White to play again. Can you see how he can threaten a checkmate which Black cannot stop?

PUZZLE 4.

Black's King and Queen are on the same line. Can White take advantage of this with an X-Ray attack?

## 5 The King

Since the whole object of the game is to capture your opponent's King, the King is the most important piece on the board. Lose him and the game is lost. When you compare him with the Rooks ranging all over the board, the Bishops gliding the lengths of the diagonals, the Queen threatening danger in every quarter and the Knights hopping about their mischievous business, the King seems positively feeble. After all, he can only move one square at a time, albeit in any direction.

In the early stages of the game, you must make sure he is safe and must take precautions against any enemy piece that approaches him. That is why so often it is a good idea to castle as soon as possible, tucking your King away out of trouble in the corner of the board where it is easy to defend him. In the centre he is far too exposed, particularly after a few pieces have been exchanged and there are open lines into the heart of your defences. Also, it is a good idea to castle because it brings one of your Rooks into the centre of the board where he is likely to be of far more use than he is stuck in a corner.

Although the King seems weak in the early stages of the game when the first priority must be to defend him, as the game unfolds and pieces are taken, so he becomes stronger and stronger until he can be a dangerous attacking piece in his own right. In fact, it can become a positive disadvantage to leave him nestling apparently safely in the corner when there is not much left on the board apart from a few Pawns. If the Queens and Rooks in particular have been exchanged, then the King really becomes an attacking piece. He can venture out into the middle of the board again to start attacking enemy Pawns.

Even so you must still be careful. As you will see, it does not take many pieces to give a quick and surprising checkmate.

There's one more rule which we have to talk about here. You know that if the King is in check and can't move out of check then it's called checkmate and the game is over. But what happens if you're *not* in check, but can't move anything without putting yourself into check? That sounds terrible, but actually it's very pleasant. If this happens, it's called 'Stalemate' and the game is a draw, with nobody winning. Look at the diagram: Black to move is not in check, so it can't be checkmate. If he moves his Bishop, he's in check from the White Rook, so that's not possible. He can't move his King forward because d7, e7 and f7 are all under control by the White King. And he can't move to f8, because that square is on the end of the diagonal from the White Queen. Black has no legal move. He is in Stalemate and the game is immediately called a draw. When you are trying to checkmate your opponent and he has only one or two pieces left, don't let him get out with a draw by Stalemate. Checkmate and Stalemate are very close to each other, but a win and a draw are a long way apart.

Stalemates usually happen when there are only a few pieces left on the board. But it's also possible to be stalemated with many men around. Look at the crazy position opposite. All the pieces are still on the board. It's White's move, and he's not in check, but he really can't move anything. All the Pawns are blocked and all the pieces either totally gummed up or pinned to the King. He can't do anything without putting himself in check. It is stalemate and the game is a draw. Of course you would have to be a very strange player to reach such a position – but in chess anything is possible.

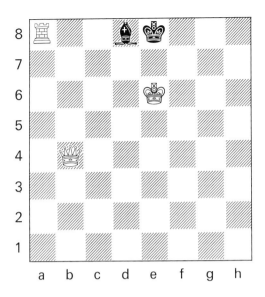

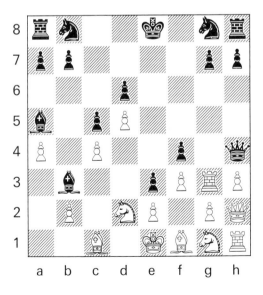

Here is an example of how you can really use your King actively, once the dangerous pieces have been exchanged. Look at this position. Both sides have just a King and a Pawn. What they want to do is push the Pawn to the far end of the board where it can become a Queen. White is to move, and his Pawn is already only two squares from coronation. Unfortunately, though, Black's King is only too ready to stop it and eat it up. After 1 c6–c7 Black just plays 1 . . . Ka6–b7 and next move he takes the Pawn. So perhaps White should think about stopping the Black Pawn. But how? His King is three squares behind it, so the Pawn will easily win the race. It looks bad for White, but he can save the game by clever moves with his King:

1 Kh8–g7! h5–h4

2 Kg7–f6! Ka6–b6 (ready to take the Pawn. The White King was getting close enough to defend it)

3 Kf6–e5 h4–h3 (after 3 . . . Kb6xc6 White plays 4 Ke5–f4 and catches the Black Pawn)

4 Ke5–d6! h3–h2

5 c6–c7 Kb6–b7

6 Kd6–d7 h2–h1=Q

7 c7–c8=Q+ Both sides have Queens and the game will be drawn.

Do you see how clever the White King has been? By moving diagonally up the board, he was able to chase the Black Pawn and help his own Pawn at the same time. In chess the shortest distance between two points is not always a straight line – the diagonal journey can be just as good or even better.

And if you still don't think the King is a useful piece, look at this position. White's King on h1 can hold out against Black's extra Bishop and Pawn. He can happily move to g2 and back again for ever. If Black brings his own King too close – to h3, g3 or f2 when White is on h1, it will always be Stalemate. The black-squared Bishop can never drive White out of his White-squared defensive retreat. The game is a draw – the King holds everything.

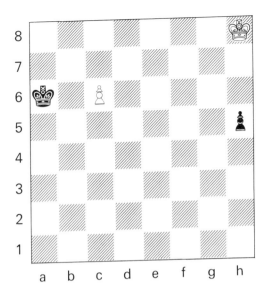

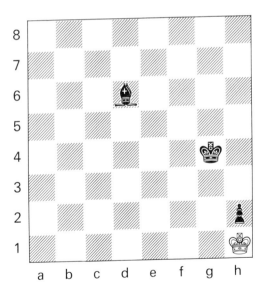

## The King – Puzzles

PUZZLE 1.

White's King and Pawn have no
moves. If only he did not have
the Rook it would be stalemate
and he would escape. So what
did White play?

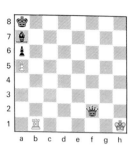

PUZZLE 2.

Black has three extra Pawns and
was expecting to win this game.
But White's next move forced an
immediate draw. What did he
play?

PUZZLE 3.

White's Pawn is only one square
from becoming a new Queen, but
it cannot advance now, and Black
seems sure to take it with his
Rook next move. How did White
save the game?

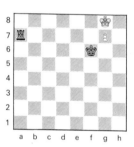

PUZZLE 4.

How can White make sure of
winning the last Black Pawn?
Take care with your King moves!

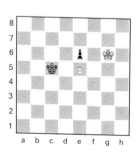

46

## 6 The Pawn

When you set the board up, it does not look as if the Pawn is really a very important piece. You have eight of them; it seems at first that they stop your powerful pieces like the Rooks from getting into the game; generally, you may have the feeling that it would be no bad idea to rid yourself of a few of them and that it does not matter if you lose a couple more than your opponent. Resist such thoughts. There are many games in which pieces are exchanged wholesale and, when the dust finally settles, one player finds himself with the apparently trivial advantage of just one Pawn more than his opponent, and from that position goes on to win.

The reason why every single Pawn should be treasured is that, although they start off as humble pieces advancing one square at a time up the board, every Pawn has the possibility of reaching that magic eighth rank and becoming a Queen.

Pawns are so special that they have a number of rules all to themselves. They are the only pieces which can become something else; they are the only pieces which cannot move backwards; the only pieces which take diagonally instead of straight ahead. There are also two other special moves. On their first move, they can go two squares instead of one; and they also have the strange ability to do what is called 'taking *en passant*' which will be explained later.

Apart from the long-term possibility of becoming a Queen, Rook, Bishop or Knight in the later stages of a game, Pawns also have an essential job to do in the early skirmishes. Actually it is two tasks. As they march forward at the start of the game, they conquer territory for the other pieces to occupy later, and at the same time, they prevent the opposition from conquering territory. This idea of controlling space is almost as important as the idea of attacking the opposing King directly, because your pieces need plenty of room if they are to attack effectively. It is the Pawns that gain that room, so care for them and they will care for you.

The Pawn has another special rule called the *en passant* capture, which is a way of capturing another Pawn quite different from all other captures on the chessboard. *En passant* means while passing, and that's just how this special rule works. Look at the position opposite: Black decides to move his Pawn forward. As the Pawn has not yet moved, it has the choice between advancing one or two squares. After *b7–b6*, White can just take it normally: *c5xb6*. The new rule comes if Black plays 1 . . . *b7–b5* because then White is allowed to take it all the same, just as if it had moved only one square forward. In fact, White captures the Pawn on b6, just as if it had never reached b5 at all. White moves his Pawn to b6 and removes the Black Pawn from b5. This is the only capture on the chessboard which can be made by moving a piece to an empty square.

Remember an *en passant* capture can only be made by a Pawn capturing another Pawn which has just moved two squares, and only if the capturing Pawn could have taken it had it moved just one square. And it is only allowed on the move immediately after the enemy Pawn has advanced. You can't wait until next move, or you lose the chance. Don't forget the *en passant* rule. It doesn't happen very often, but it can be useful.

The other rule specially for Pawns, which makes them so much stronger than they look, is the possibility to promote a Pawn into any other piece of its own colour (except the King, of course) if the Pawn reaches the end of the board. You can even have nine Queens on the board at the same time if you manage to advance all eight Pawns through to the end. But remember, you don't have to promote to a Queen. Another piece may sometimes be even better. Set up the position opposite on your board. If White pushes his Pawn to c8 and claims a Queen, it would be stalemate. A draw! Look how the Black King would then have no squares. But 1 *c7–c8=R!* leaves Black with just one move: 1 . . . *Ka7–a6* and now comes 2 *Rc8–a8* mate! Usually the Queen is the strongest piece, but sometimes a Rook, Knight or Bishop might be better.

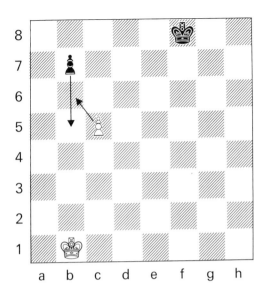

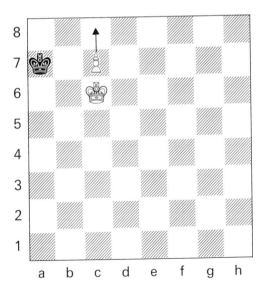

Once a Pawn starts racing towards the end of the board, it becomes very dangerous. If there are no Pawns of the opposite colour blocking its way on its own file, and none of the next-door files which could capture it when it advances, then it has a clear road ahead to the queening square. Such a Pawn is called a *Passed Pawn*. Obtaining a passed pawn is the first stage in getting a new Queen.

Set up the position opposite on your chessboard. Just three Pawns each and nobody has any passed Pawns, but White can win with a clever idea. He plays 1 *b5–b6!* which threatens to take the Black Pawns on a7 or c7. So Black must himself capture this bold Pawn: 1 . . . *c7xb6*. White now doesn't recapture, but pushes another Pawn: 2 *a5–a6!* Black must take again, or White will capture on b7, so he plays 2 . . . *b7xa6*, but now comes 3 *c5–c6!* and White has his passed Pawn with nothing to stop its coronation to Queen in two more moves. After *c6–c7* and *c7–c8=Q* the extra White Queen will win the game. Now go back to the beginning when White played 1 *b5–b6!* What would have happened if Black took with the other Pawn: 1 . . . *a7xb6*. Then it's just the same thing but the other way round: 2 *c5–c6! b7xc6* 3 *a5–a6* and again nothing can stop the Pawn from becoming a new Queen. You should look very carefully at this idea to see how White gave up two Pawns just to force a passed Pawn which could not be stopped. It's good practice playing games just with the Kings and eight Pawns each; then you learn just what these modest pieces can really do.

Don't forget that a Pawn can also sometimes be a strong attacking piece on its own. Set up the position opposite. White to move has only one Pawn and it can't even move. Black is ready to gain a new Queen, but it's the White Pawn which wins the game. White plays 1 *Rg3–h3+!*. The Rook is protected by the Pawn so can't be taken by the King. Black must play 1 . . . *Be6xh3* and now comes 2 *g2–g3!* and it's checkmate. White's King and Pawn win the game, with just a little help from the Black pieces.

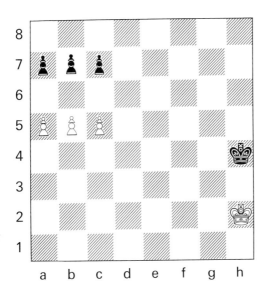

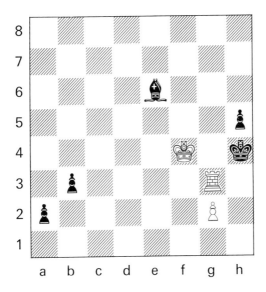

## The Pawn – Puzzles

PUZZLE 1.

Black is in check from the Bishop on f4. He played 1 . . . g7–g5, said 'check' himself and felt happy. Was he right?

PUZZLE 2.

White to play looks ready to get a new Queen? Would that be right, or should he do something else?

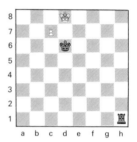

PUZZLE 3.

How can White create a passed Pawn which the Black King cannot stop from reaching the end and becoming a Queen?

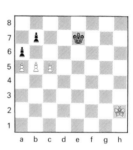

PUZZLE 4.

Should White push one of his Pawns, or is it safer to come to g2 with his King first?

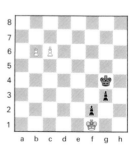

# THREE: Strategy and Tactics

## 1 The Opening

Now you know what the pieces can do, the question is how do you get them into positions where they can be most effective and dangerous.

At the beginning of the game, the two armies face one another with all the heavy pieces behind their Pawns and a no-man's-land of four whole ranks of open space between them. At the beginning of the game, there are two things to think about: first, you must think about slowly advancing your Pawn front so that you have enough room for all your men to operate efficiently; second, you must get your pieces out on to squares where they can actively join in the game.

At first your pieces should head towards the middle of the board. You do not know what your opponent is going to do, but as he brings his men into play you will begin to see what his intentions are. For instance, you will see where his King intends to stay and what pieces of yours he intends to attack. So you want all your men to be ready to go wherever they might be needed. The nearer the middle of the board they are, the more quickly they can move to where danger threatens.

In the opening, you should try to bring out all your pieces as quickly as possible. An attack with just one or two pieces can easily be stopped, so you need all of them in play. This leads to a very important general rule. In the early stages try not to move each piece more than once. And try not to lose time by letting your opponent chase your pieces around while he is playing useful moves himself. So don't bring your Queen out too early; don't make more Pawn moves than will allow your pieces out; as a general rule, try to get your Knights into the game before the Bishops, and try to get one Rook into the middle of the board, and therefore into the game, by castling. Getting your pieces out is called 'development'. When you have castled, all your men are actively placed and your development is completed. Then the opening is over.

Now let's look at the opening of a game to see what sort of things can happen, and what can go wrong if you do not treat your pieces properly.

1 e2–e4     e7–e5

Moving the e-Pawn forward is the most common first move. It prepares to bring out both Queen and Bishop. And the e-Pawn also claims some space in the centre of the board.

2 Bf1–c4     Nb8–c6
3 Qd1–h5     (see diagram)

Watch out. White is trying a Scholar's Mate. He wants to play 3 Qh5xf7 mate.

3 . . .          g7–g6

But Black sees the threat. Now the White Queen is attacked by the Pawn, which has stepped in the way of her attack to f7. Notice that the Pawn on e5 is also protected – by the Knight on c6.

4 Qh5–f3

Again White wants to play 5 Qf3xf7 mate.

4 . . .          Ng8–f6

Once again, stepping in the way of the threat.

5 Qf3–b3

Another idea – Queen and Bishop line up on the same diagonal to threaten 6 Bb3xf7+. But White is really moving his Queen around too much. When is he going to get his other pieces out?

5 . . .          Qd8–e7!

Black defends f7 with Queen and King, so White cannot capture. Meanwhile Black threatens to take the White e-Pawn with his Knight on f6. So White defends it.

6 d2–d3     Nc6–d4!     (see diagram)

Now Black starts to develop threats of his own. Just look at that beautiful central Knight. It attacks the White Queen (remember what we said about chasing round Queens brought out too early) and also attacks the Pawn on c2. If Black can take this Pawn safely he will be forking the White King and Rook. That's a very common way to lose a Rook in the corner.

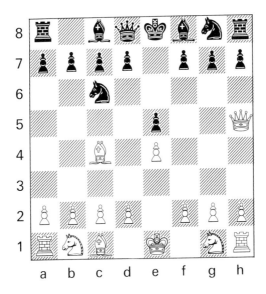

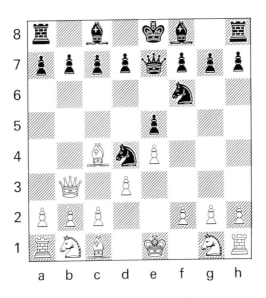

7 *Qb3–a4    c7–c6*

White moves his Queen where it still protects c2, but now Black has found something else to threaten. Do you see the idea of his Pawn move? He wants to play b7–b5 attacking the White Queen and Bishop at the same time. A Pawn fork! The Pawn on c6 will protect the Pawn on b5 to stop the Bishop taking it.

8 *Bc4–b3    a7–a5!*

You'll see the reason for this clever move later.

9 *Ng1–h3    b7–b5!*   (*see diagram*)

Just look at the position now. White's Queen, which he thought was attacking so fiercely, is now threatened by a mere Pawn. And she only has one square to go to where she cannot be taken by a Pawn.

10 *Qa4–a3    Qe7–d8!*

A lovely move, going back home with the Queen. Now the Black Bishop on f8 attacks the poor White Queen. This was a discovered attack. The Black Queen moved out of the way to discover a deadly attack.

11 *Bb3xf7 +*

A really desperate remedy. White's Queen is so bottled up by Black's advanced Pawns that she has nowhere to go.

11 . . . .    *Ke8xf7*

12 *Qa3–c3*

Well, White has lost his Bishop, but at least the Queen is now out of trouble. Or is she?

12 . . .    *Bf8–b4!* (*see diagram*).

And after all that, the Bishop pin still wins the Queen. With Black Bishop, White Queen and White King all on the same diagonal, White loses his Queen. A just punishment for all those Queen moves early on in the game, when he should have been getting the other pieces out.

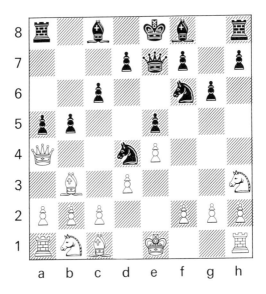

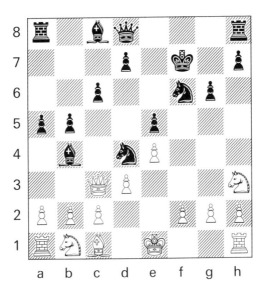

The aim of the opening is to get all your pieces into play as quickly as possible, so here are some more words of advice to help you decide where to put them.

You should start the game with some idea of where you would like to bring out your pieces. Since you don't really know anything about where your opponent is going to put his men, it's a good idea to keep yours as centrally placed as possible, just to be ready for anything. So, for example, you might decide that you would like to play the centre Pawns forward to e4 and d4, bring the Knights to f3 and c3, Bishops to c4 and f4, castle K-side and finally put the Rook on e1. That would be a good plan, leaving everything ready for the middle game. But your opponent has moves too and these will interfere with your plans. So, for example, if you start with 1 *e2–e4* and he plays 1 . . . *e7–e5*, already his first move has covered the d4 and f4 squares to make it harder for you to carry out your plan of putting a Pawn on d4 and Bishop on f4. Already you have to change plans a little. Perhaps you can decide that the Bishop is now better on e3, and the Pawn will be happier on d3. But all the time, although you only play one move at a time, you will have an idea of where all the other pieces are going.

Always try to play actively, attacking your opponent's undefended pieces. Then he has to spend time moving them out of the way, or defending them. After 1 *e2–e4 e7–e5*, the most common move, even in World Championship play, is 2 *Ng1–f3*, bringing a piece into play and attacking the Pawn on e5.

Finally, you must always look at what your opponent is doing. His moves might be attacking some of your pieces, or he might have just made a mistake which lets you win something. Keep your eyes open for danger and for attacking chances. Mistakes can happen right at the start of a game. Make sure it's your opponent who makes them!

## 2 The Middle Game

This is where the real fascination of chess begins. There are masses of books about the openings, there are well-known theories you can learn quite quickly so that you can play quite a lot of moves without having to think very hard about them. But in the middle game you are on your own. That is why you sometimes read that a player took as long as an hour pondering about what he should do next.

So there you are: all your men are in play; you have castled, so your King is safe. Now what do you do next?

This is when you begin to think about the attack which is going to win the game for you, but you must also plan this attack very carefully and prepare for it by assembling your pieces where you want them. At the same time, you must remember that your opponent is trying to do the same to you, so even while you are preparing your winning attack, you must keep an eye on defence so that your opponent cannot execute his winning attack. Nothing is more annoying than being two moves away from a spectacular checkmate only to find that you have overlooked a weakness and are checkmated yourself!

You must keep on the look-out for the little tactical traps you've already met – the pins, the forks, the attacks which win or lose pieces. You might easily win a game thanks to a pin or fork and you will be quite right to feel jolly pleased with yourself for having seen and taken advantage of the opportunity. But as you get better, these chances become rarer because your opponents will have become better at seeing the threats and avoiding them. Also, a pin or fork only uses one of your pieces.

What the middle game does is to give you the chance to use all your pieces together, to launch such an overwhelming attack that at the end there is nothing your opponent can do except capitulate more or less gracefully. To win a game with a trap like a pin or a fork is clever; to win a game by using all your men together in an irresistible middle-game attack is a triumph which will give you something to gloat about (to yourself, of course) for a very long time.

Now let's see an example of how you can make plans for the middle-game and carry them out successfully. We'll look at a game won by the great English player Joseph Blackburne in 1901. He had the Black pieces, and the opening moves were 1 e2–e4 e7–e5 2 d2–d4 e5xd4 3 Qd1xd4 Nb8–c6 4 Qd4–e3 g7–g6 5 Bc1–d2 Bf8–g7 6 Nb1–c3 Ng8–e7 7 0–0–0 0–0, reaching the position shown opposite. With his last move, White has given away his plan. Before White castled, Black had no idea where the White King was going to spend the middle-game. Now he knows that White wants to attack on the King's side (that means the side where both Kings started the game) with his own King tucked away on the other side of the board. Black has now castled too and must start thinking about how he can attack the White King. Let's see what happened:

8 f2–f4     d7–d5!

Black must finish developing his pieces before he can start to attack. So far only his Bishop on g7 is pointing towards the White King. This Pawn move prepares to bring out the other Bishop.

9 e4xd5     Nc6–b4

Rather than recapture the Pawn with his Knight on e7, Black moves his other Knight. Note how this Knight is now looking menacingly at a2, c2 and d5.

10 Bf1–c4     Bc8–f5

Now Black has both Bishops and a Knight pointing in the direction of the White King. This developing move adds to the attack on c2, now threatened twice and defended only once – by the White King.

11 Bc4–b3

White defends the attacked c-Pawn with his Bishop.

11 . . .     Ne7xd5
12 Nc3xd5     Nb4xd5
13 Qe3–f3     Qd8–f6!     (see diagram)

White was attacking the Knight with both Queen and Bishop. Black has replied with an even stronger threat. He wants to play 14 . . . Qf6xb2 mate! Look how Queen and Bishop line up to create this attacking chance.

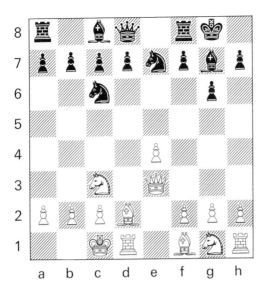

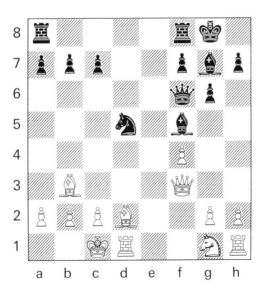

14 c2–c3

White defends by blocking the diagonal.

14 . . .        Nd5–b4!

Another piece joins the attack. See how the Knight cannot be taken: after 15 c3xb4 the diagonal is open again and Black mates with 15 . . . Qf6xb2.

15 Bb3–c4

The Black Knight was heading for a check on d3, so White defends that square.

15 . . .        Qf6–a6! (see diagram)

A brilliant move! The Queen attacks the Bishop on its own diagonal, but can't she be captured? The answer is no! After 16 Bc4xa6, Black has a beautiful mate with 16 . . . Nb4xa2! The Bishop on f5 covers the c2 and b1 squares, giving the White King no escape.

16 g2–g4

White attacks the troublesome Bishop, hoping to drive it away.

16 . . .        Qa6xa2!

Another tremendous attacking move. The Queen can still not be taken: 17 Bc4xa2 Nb4xa2 is mate again. But also Black threatens both Qa2–a1 mate and Qa2–b1 mate.

17 Bd2–e3

White gets the Bishop out of the way to give his King an escape on d2.

17 . . .        Bg7xc3!

Just look at all those Black pieces attacking the White King. Now the threat of Qa2xb2 mate is added to White's troubles. He can't take the Bishop on c3 since 18 b2xc3 opens the way for Black to play 18 . . . Qa2–c2 mate. He no longer has any defence.

18 Bc4xa2  Nb4xa2 mate! (see diagram)

A beautiful checkmate. The Knight gives check and the two Bishops combine to cover all the squares round the White King. Note how White never managed to bring his King's Knight or Rook into the game. And Black never needed his Rooks at all. Black's middle-game plan to attack the King was carried out to its logical conclusion – checkmate!

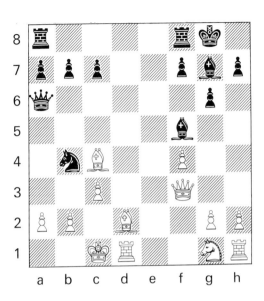

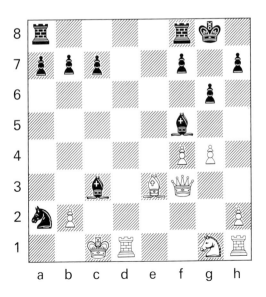

It's your move and you've brought all your pieces into play. What do you do now? Always start by looking very carefully at your opponent's last move. Why has he played it? What does the piece he just moved do now, which it was not doing before? Look out for any attacks on your pieces by the piece he moved. And be especially careful to watch out also for any discovered attacks. It's very easy to overlook an attack from a piece which was hiding behind the one which moved.

Perhaps your opponent has just made a bad move. Has he overlooked something you were threatening? Does his last move give you the chance to win anything, either by a direct capture or by a fork or pin?

If you decide that you are not in any immediate danger, and you can't win anything quickly, then you just have to improve your position. Look at all your pieces and ask yourself what they are all doing. Usually you will be quite happy that some are working actively, but others are just sitting around doing nothing in particular. Think about how to make these inactive pieces work harder. Find better squares for them, where they will be able to join in the job of making life more difficult for your opponent's pieces.

And remember that in playing chess you must always be very patient. You can't win a game without your opponent making mistakes, and you can't lose one without making mistakes yourself. Tartakower once said that the mistakes are all there, just waiting to be made. Your job is to make sure that you don't make them yourself, and you do notice when your opponent makes one.

# 3 The Endgame

The more you play chess and the better you become, the more you will realise that overwhelming middle-game attacks that smash your opponent are comparatively rare. What happens much more often is that there is a grim struggle during the middle game with pieces being swopped off until eventually one or other of you is left with perhaps only a minute advantage.

When there are only a few pieces left on the board and, because there are few chances of checkmating attacks, the Kings feel safe to venture out from wherever they have been hiding, we have reached what is called 'the endgame'. Now obviously, if both of you have only a King left on the board, neither of you can win because neither of you can checkmate the opposition King. So when you approach the endgame, you need to know what the minimum force is that can checkmate the other King, and how you actually execute checkmate.

A King and Queen, King and Rook, King and two Bishops or King, Bishop and Knight can all win against a King, but King and Bishop alone or King and Knight cannot force mate. It may seem odd that a Knight can give a smothered mate on its own when the enemy King is surrounded by his own men, but cannot mate on an empty board even with the help of his King.

The only way to learn how to win with these pieces is to practise, so put a King and single Bishop or Knight on a board against a King. What you will find is that there is no checkmate, but there are some stalemates – and in the endgame that is something you must pay special attention to. Nothing is more irritating than to have a winning position, to move all your pieces in for the kill, and then find that your opponent has discovered a stalemate; it's a terrible way of throwing away a win!

As you play through endgame positions, you will gradually realise why in the chapter about Pawns you kept on being told to care for them and not throw them away with gay abandon. A Pawn can become a truly formidable piece in the subtleties of winning an endgame position.

If you are left with King and one or two pieces against King, the idea is always the same: you restrict the opponent's King to a part of the board, then drive him further and further back, finally checkmating on the edge of the board when he can retreat no further. The ending with two Rooks against King shows this plan in action very clearly. From the position shown, White starts with 1 *Rh2–h4* to cover the whole of the fourth rank. As long as this Rook stays there, the Black King is confined to the back half of the board. Play continues 1 . . . *Kd5–e5* and now 2 *Rg1–g5+*. The King must retreat: 2 . . . *Ke5–f6* and now 3 *Rg5–a5* threatens Rh4–h6+ forcing him still further back. Black plays 3 . . . *Kf6–g6* but after 4 *Rh4–b4* the Rooks are safe from attack by the King and the rest is easy: 4 *Kg6–f6* 5 *Rb4–b6+ Kf6–e7* 6 *Ra5–a7+ Ke7–d8* 7 *Rb6–b8 checkmate*. Make sure you understand this method clearly. All the time one Rook has the task of cutting off the King and preventing its advance, then the other gives check to force it further back.

Giving mate with King and one Rook against King is much slower, but also not really hard. This time you must use the King to help. Start with the same position as above, but remove the Rook from g1. Again White begins with 1 *Rh2–h4* with the same idea as before – cutting off the King from the front half of the board. Now watch the procedure, slow but sure, in the following moves: 1 . . . *Kd5–e5* 2 *Ka1–b2 Ke5–d5* 3 *Kb2–c3 Kd5–e5* 4 *Kc3–d3 Ke5–d5* 5 *Rh4–h5+!* (*see diagram*). This is the fundamental position for forcing back. White's King prevents the Black King from moving forwards. 5 . . .*Kd5–e6* 6 *Kd3–d4 Ke6–f6*      7 *Kd4–e4 Kf6–g6*      8 *Rh5–a5 Kg6–f6* 9 *Ra5–b5* (just waiting) *Kf6–g6* 10 *Ke4–f4* (following, so that 10 . . . Kg6–f6 is met by 11 Ra5–a6+) 10 . . . *Kg6–h6* 11 *Kf4–g4 Kh6–g6* 12 *Ra5–a6+! Kg6–f7* 13 *Kg4–f5 Kf7–e7* 14 *Kf5–e5 Ke7–d7* 15 *Ra6–h6 Kd7–c7* 16 *Ke5–d5 Kc7–b7* 17 *Kd5–c5 Kb7–c7* 18 *Rh6–h7+! Kc7–d8* 19 *Kc6–d6 Kd8–c8* 20 *Rh7–g7 Kc8–b8* 21 *Kd6–c6 Kb8–a8* 22 *Kc6–b6 Ka8–b8* 23 *Rg7–g8 mate*. Note how White just repeats the same idea until it's finally checkmate.

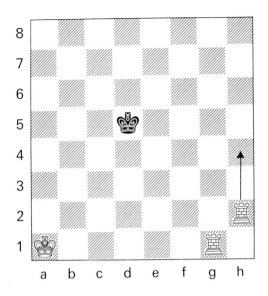

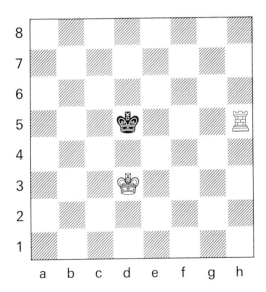

Of course, King and Queen against King is even easier; the Queen covers even more squares than the Rook, but again she needs the help of her King to give checkmate. You do just have to be a little more careful not to get too confident and give stalemate by accident.

The mate with King and two Bishops against King is more difficult, but the principle is the same: squeeze the King back to the edge first, then force mate. In the position shown we see the Bishops at their best. Next to each other, they restrict the King to the triangle behind their diagonals. Watch the procedure from now on: 1 Ke2–f3 Ke6–d6 2 Kf3–f4 Kd6–e6 3 Bd4–e5! (Draw the Bishops' diagonals and you'll see that the triangle has shrunk) 3 . . . Ke6–e7 4 Be4–d5 Ke7–d7 5 Kf4–f5 Kd7–e7 6 Bd5–e6 Ke7–d8 7 Be5–d6 Kd8–e8. The King has been forced to the back – but to mate it we'll need to get it into the corner: 8 Kf5–f6 Ke8–d8 9 Be6–f5 (waiting) Kd8–e8 10 Bd6–c7! (Taking d8 away from Black. Note that 10 Bd6–e7?? was stalemate!) 10 . . . Ke8–f8 11 Bf5–d7! (and now e8 has been removed from Black) Kf8–g8 12 Kf6–g6 Kg8–f8 13 Bc7–d6+ Kf8–g8 14 Bd7–e6+ Kg8–h8 15 Bd6–e5 mate! Note how White only gives check right at the end of this process. Often it's more important just gradually to take squares away from the enemy King than to try to force him to move by checking.

King, Bishop and Knight alone against King can also force mate, but this one is much more difficult. Again you can force the King back to the edge, but then you discover that you can only mate him in the corner which is the same colour as your Bishop. From the diagram opposite, here is the end of the long procedure: 1 Bf4–c7 (taking away d8 from Black to force his King towards h8) 1 . . . Ke8–f8 2 Bc7–b6 (waiting) Kf8–e8 3 Nf5–d6+ Ke8–f8 4 Ke6–f6 Kf8–g8 5 Kf6–g6 Kg8–f8 6 Bb6–d8 (Now e8 and e7 are barred) Kf8–g8 7 Bd8–e7 Kg8–h8 8 Nd6–f5 Kh8–g8 9 Nf5–h6+ Kg8–h8 10 Be7–f6 mate.

You should know too that King and two Knights alone cannot force mate, unless your opponent is very helpful.

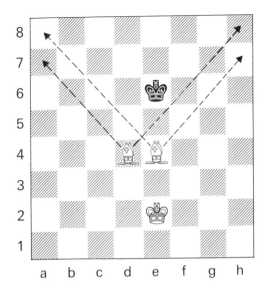

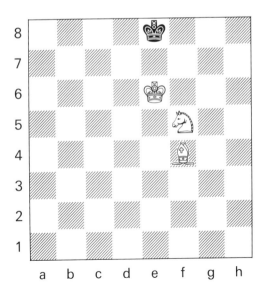

Lastly, before we leave the Endgame, we should see how King and one Pawn can sometimes win against King. Of course, if your opponent's King is a long way away from your Pawn, you'll win by just pushing the Pawn as fast as it can go and he won't be able to stop it turning into a Queen, but sometimes, even if he can get his King right in front of the Pawn, you might still be able to win.

Set up the position opposite on your board and think about what you would play if you were Black and it was your turn to move. Where to put the King? We'll see that it makes a great difference where you choose. Try 1 . . . Ke7–d8. Then comes 2 Ke5–d6 Kd8–e8 3 e6–e7 Ke8–f7 4 Kd6–d7! and next move the Pawn will become a Queen. The same happens after 1 . . . Ke7–f8 2 Ke5–f6 Kf6–e8 3 e6–e7 Ke8–d7 4 Kf6–f7. So is Black losing this position? We should try the last remaining move 1 . . . Ke7–e8! and now 2 Ke5–d6 Ke8–d8 3 e6–e7+ Kd8–e8 4 Kd6–e6 only gives stalemate, and the same after 2 Ke5–f6 Ke8–f8! 3 e6–e7+ Kf8–e8 4 Kf6–e6 (other moves just lose the Pawn). So Black can in fact draw this game, but see how careful he must be!

Now look at the second diagram. Rather similar, except the White King is in front of his Pawn. What happens now? Suppose it is Black's move. 1 . . . Ke7–f7 2 Ke5–d6! Kf7–e8 3 Kd6–e6! Ke8–d8 4 Ke6–f7! followed by pushing the Pawn straight home to become a Queen. The King protects e6, e7 and e8, so the Black King cannot defend. Look how the White King dances with the Black one, just to make room for his Pawn to advance.

But what if it's White's move in the same position. That makes all the difference and Black can draw! After 1 Ke5–d5 Ke7–d7! the Black King prevents White's from advancing. 2 Kd5–e5 Kd7–e7 3 Ke5–f5 Ke7–f7! 4 e4–e5 Kf7–e7 5 e5–e6 Ke7–e8! and we are back in the drawn position from earlier: 6 Kf5–f6 Ke8–f8 7 e6–e7+ Kf8–e8 8 Kf6–e6 stalemate. This is such a delicate endgame that it even matters whose move it is in any position. Study these examples and learn the ideas; they can easily gain you those important extra half-points.

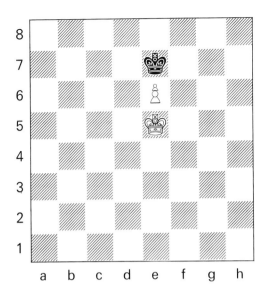

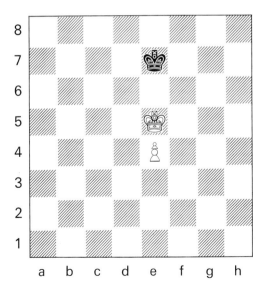

## 1  Use Your King

There is no clear moment when the middle game ends and the endgame begins. The real difference comes when the Kings are no longer in danger and can safely wander out into the open board. So, if it's safe, bring your King up the board to attack your opponent's Pawns and to help your own plans. A King can be worth about the same as a Knight or Bishop if it is allowed to play, so don't keep it tucked away uselessly when it can join the game.

## 2  Attack Your Opponent's Pawns

Never make the mistake of thinking that Pawns are too small to be worth bothering about. Especially in the endgame they can be very important indeed. They are also not very good at running away from attack, so threaten your opponent's Pawns when you can.

## 3  Keep Your Pieces Active

As the board becomes emptier, more and more lines become open and Bishops and Rooks have more and more room. So it is very important to use their possibilities. If your pieces have to defend, they will not be joining properly in the game. So make sure that your Rooks and Bishops are attacking and your opponent's are defending. When your opponent's King is still on its back rank, your Rook can be very well placed on the rank in front. From there it will attack his unmoved Pawns as well as preventing his King from moving forward. This 'Rook on the Seventh' can be a decisive advantage in an Endgame.

## 4  Push your Passed Pawns

The nearer a Pawn gets to the end of the board, the closer it is to becoming another Queen, so push those passed Pawns if you want to win!

## 4 Planning

A chess game consists of the opening, the middle game and the endgame. But it is not like a boxing match where the bell goes at the end of each round and it is often difficult to tell exactly where one part of the game ends and the next begins. However, they should all fit together, one leading logically on to another. You cannot sit down and plan a game like that, though. What you can do is have long-term plans and short-term plans.

Long-term planning is bound to be vague. You might have a general idea about what you want to do, but so has your opponent and, as you hope he does not know your plan, so you do not know his. You may have to change your plans to cope with an unexpected threat or to take advantage of a mistake. So, as the pieces come into play during the opening, you should begin to think about what you will be trying to do later; where you will attack, what you should be worried about.

Short-term planning is simpler. With each move either you or your opponent make, the position will change and your plans may have to change too. Look carefully at each of his moves. Ask yourself why he did it, what is he threatening, where can he go from his new square, has he uncovered an attack from another piece, what difference does it make to what you want to do.

Very often you will not be able to think of anything much to do. Everything looks even and balanced and there are no obvious opportunities for attack. So, do not start an attack; if the position is as even as you think it is, there is no guarantee that any attack of yours will succeed. Instead of attacking, try simply to put your pieces on squares where they control more territory or co-operate better with each other or strengthen your defences. Put them on squares where they simply look better.

In a good game, all the moves will fit logically together to form part of your plan. In the opening you put your men where you think they are going to be useful; in the middle game you start to use them; and in the endgame you finish things off and gain the reward of victory for your hard work.

Let's look at a complete game to see how the ideas should be carried out. This is a game won by the great American Paul Morphy. It was played in Paris in 1859, in fact in a box at the Paris Opéra. Morphy had the White pieces while as Black the Duke of Brunswick and Count Isouard decided their moves together.

1 e2–e4      e7–e5
2 Ng1–f3    d7–d6

Black defends his attacked Pawn. This move lets the Bishop out from c8, but shuts in the other one, which can now only go as far as e7.

3 d2–d4      Bc8–g4   (see diagram)

Black pins the Knight on f3. If it moves, he will take the Queen with his Bishop.

4 d4xe5      Bg4xf3

A necessary exchange; after 4 . . . d6xe5, White exchanges Queens with 5 Qd1xd8+ Ke8xd8, then accepts the Pawn with 6 Nf3xe5 – the pin has vanished.

5 Qd1xf3    d6xe5
6 Bf1–c4

Already White has two pieces developed; Black has yet to start.

6 . . .      Ng8–f6
7 Qf3–b3!   (see diagram)

White uses his extra move to begin the attack. He threatens both 8 Bc4xf7+ and 8 Qb3xb7. Black cannot defend both.

7 . . .         Qd8–e7

Black hopes now for 8 Qb3xb7 when he will be able to exchange Queens with 8 . . . Qe7–b4+! 9 Qb7xb4 Bf8xb4+. Morphy decides instead just to continue with his development, leaving Black's Queen gumming up his Bishop.

8 Nb1–c3    c7–c6

Now defending the b7 Pawn with his Queen.

9 Bc1–g5!

An important pin to constrict Black further. See how White brings out all his pieces actively.

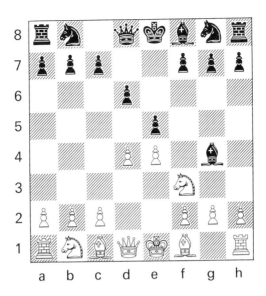

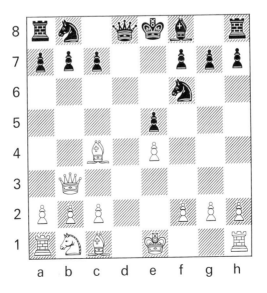

9 . . .      b7–b5   (see diagram)

Black attacks the Bishop on c4, trying to drive it from the diagonal leading to his vulnerable Pawn on f7.

10 Nc3xb5!

Giving up this Knight to trap the Black King in the middle of the board. White's whole Opening play has been designed to delay Black's development; now he starts to take advantage of his own active men.

10 . . .      c6xb5
11 Bc4xb5 +Nb8–d7
12 0–0–0!

Castling is not just a King move; here the Rook comes immediately to the open d-file to bring more pressure against the pinned Knight on d7. Remember this Knight is not really protected effectively by his friend on f6, for that too is pinned by a White Bishop. So the Knight needs another defender.

12 . . .      Ra8–d8
13 Rd1xd7! Rd8xd7
14 Rh1–d1

One Rook left d1 just to let the other take its place. Meanwhile all that has happened on Black's side is that the pinned Knight on d7 has become a pinned Rook. Now with Bishop on f8 and Rook on h8 unable to join the game, Black is running out of reinforcements to come to the defence.

14 . . .      Qe7–e6

At least the Knight is now unpinned, but already White can win brilliantly.

15 Bb5xd7 +Nf6xd7
16 Qb3–b8 + !

A nice deflection; just to get the Knight out of the way.

16 . . .      Nd7xb8
17 Rd1–d8 mate! (see diagram)

With his last two men, White delivers mate. A beautifully logical attack from start to finish.

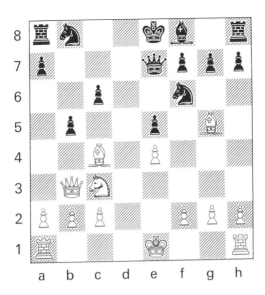

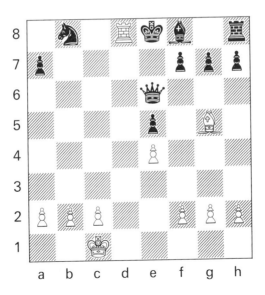

# FOUR: Sacrifices and Brilliancies

Trying not to lose your own pieces and hoping to capture your opponent's is the usual rule while playing chess, but sometimes you can win a game by deliberately giving up one or more of your men. When you lose a piece on purpose, usually to force a quick checkmate or to win back more men later in the game, it is called a sacrifice. Some international tournaments have special prizes for the best game won with brilliant, surprising sacrifices. They are called Brilliancy Prizes, and the brilliant games are published in chess magazines all over the world.

In the old Viennese coffee-houses where chess was played many years ago, the spectators used to admire brilliant sacrifices so much that they would shower the board with gold coins for the winner.

In this section we shall be looking at some brilliant finishes to games which might easily have won such boardfuls of gold. These are a little more complicated than most of the positions earlier in this book, so you should always set them up on your own boards and play through the moves. We have chosen six positions; in each one a different piece is the star performer.

*A The Rook*

Remember the back rank mate? This position is a beautiful example of that idea. Black's King is in that vulnerable position with the three unmoved Pawns in front of him, but how can White take advantage of it? The Rook on e8 is defended twice, so there seems to be no checkmate possibility. If only the Black Queen did not defend the Rook then 1 Re2xe8+ would force checkmate. So White played 1 *Qd4–g4!* trying to lure the Queen away from her defensive duty. Black cannot take the unprotected Queen, or Re2xe8+ will mate next move. So Black played 1 . . . *Qd7–b5* still defending the Rook. White answered 2 *Qg4–c4!!* now offering the Queen to both Queen and Rook, but both are needed for defence. The game continued 2 . . . *Qb5–d7* 3 *Qc4–c7!!* *Qd7–b5* 4 *a2–a4!* *Qb5xa4* 5 *Re2–e4!* *Qa4–b5* (The Rook could not be taken with 5 . . . Re8xe4 because of 6 Qc7xc8+ forcing another back rank mate) 6 *Qc7xb7!* The final Queen sacrifice. Black's Queen no longer has a safe square to protect the Rook. So 6 . . . *Qb5xb7* 7 *Re2xe8+ Rc8xe8* 8 *Re1xe8* checkmate.

*B The Knight*

Some brilliancies might win showers of gold coins, but this one won a World Championship. In 1978 Karpov beat Korchnoi by six wins to five in their match for the World Chess Championship. His two Knights were the heroes of this game. It's Karpov, with the Black pieces, to play:

1 . . .         *Nd2–f3+!*

and suddenly the game was over. White has only two possible moves:

2 *Kg1–h1* is answered by 2 . . . *Ne4–f2 mate!* while 2 *g2xf3* lasts just one move longer: 2 . . . *Rc6–g6+* 3 *Kg1–h1* and again 3 . . . *Ne4–f2* is checkmate.

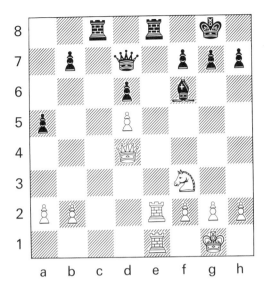

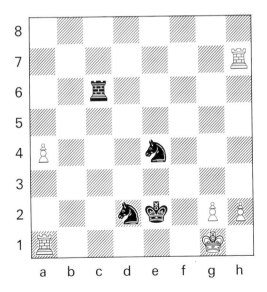

## C  The Bishop

Sacrificing a Bishop can sometimes be a good way to open attacking lines to the enemy King. Here is an example where White gives up both of his Bishops just to give his Queen and Rook the room they need. From this position White starts 1 *Bd3xh7+!* removing one of the Pawns which shelters the Black King. After 1 . . . *Kg8xh7* comes 2 *Qe2–h5+* and the King must go back: 2 . . . *Kg8–h8*. Now the other Bishop gives himself up: 3 *Bb2xg7!* White threatens Qh5–h8 mate, so Black takes this offering too: 3 . . . *Kg8xg7*. At the cost of both Bishops, White has left the Black King quite naked. A high price, but it's worth it! 4 *Qh5–g5+ Kg7–h7* (or h8, it makes no difference) 5 *Rf1–f3!* Finally a quiet move, but a killer. Nothing can stop White's next move: 6 *Rf3–h3* and the Black King will be checkmate!

## D  The Queen

We know how strong the Queen can be when she gets near the enemy King, but this White Queen looks a long way away. White's job is to bring her close without losing time. If only she could arrive at h7 the game would be over at once. Set up the position and watch what happened now:

1 *Rh1–h8+!Kg8xh8*  Black has no choice; he must take the Rook.

2 *Rd1–h1+ Kh8–g8*  Again no real choice; the King must return.

3 *Rh1–h8+!Kg8xh8*  What is White doing? He has just lost both Rooks!

4 *Qc1–h1+!Kh8–g8*

5 *Qh1–h7 checkmate!*

Finally the Queen arrives, and Black could do nothing about it. Just as the Double Bishop Sacrifice in the example above gave White's Queen and Rook the space they needed to win the game, here it was a Double Rook Sacrifice which created the room for the Queen to move over to h1 without loss of any time.

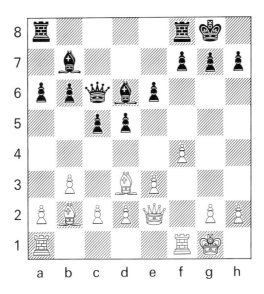

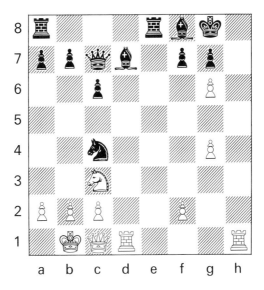

*E The King*

Black's Pawn here has only one square to go before it becomes a new Queen. If it is Black's move he plays 1 . . . Nh4–g2! That move would cut off the line of the White Bishop to h1 and let Black push his Pawn without the new Queen being taken by the Bishop. But what can White do about this threat? There seems to be nothing to stop Black's plan. But surprisingly, if it is White's move, he can still save the game.

> 1 Bb7–h1!!  Kg1xh1
> 2 Ke1–f2!!

Just look at this position. The Black King and Pawn cannot move; they are completely hemmed in by the White King. So Black must move his Knight, and any Knight move is answered by 3 Kf2–f1! White can happily spend the rest of the game playing his King to and fro between f1 and f2. The Knight can't stop him, because of its strange move which goes from white square to black square and back again. The Knight can never attack the square the White King wants to go to. But notice that 2 Ke1–f1? would have lost the game after 2 . . . Nh4–g2 3 Kf1–f2 Ng2–e3! 4 Kf2xe3 (f1 is covered by the Knight) Kh1–g1 and the Pawn is free to become a Queen.

*F The Pawn*

White must really make good use of his Pawn on b7 if he is to win this position. There is no time for slow measures, since Black threatens checks on e4 or e1 with his Queen. Look how White wins:

> 1 Rc2–c8 + ! Rh8xc8
> 2 Qb6–a7 + !!  White sets up a Knight fork, though he
> hasn't got a Knight!
> 2 . . .        Kb8xa7
> 3 b7xc8 = N!! +

And next move the new Knight takes the Black Queen then comes round to mop up the Pawns. Remember always, a Pawn does not have to become a Queen; it can promote to other pieces – and sometimes that is better.

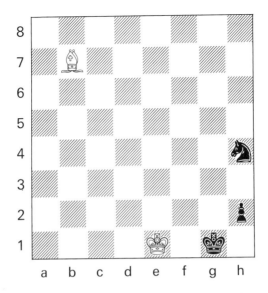

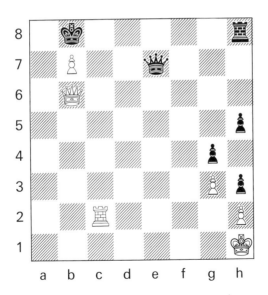

# FIVE: More About the Game

Earlier on we talked about how games can be drawn, either because neither player has enough material to force a win, or because of stalemate. In the diagram opposite, you will see another sort of draw. Black's King is in check and can only escape to h7 or h8. White's Queen can check again on h5. That is all White can do because the moment he stops giving checks, he is going to be checkmated on d1. So Black is in perpetual check, but never checkmate, and the game is drawn.

White would claim a draw by repetition of moves, but there are very similar circumstances where either player can claim a draw. If any position is exactly repeated three times with the same player to move, whether or not any checks have been given, then that too is a draw, if one of the players claims it.

Sometimes it is quite obvious that it is impossible for either player to win, but one player is too stubborn to give up. To stop them going on moving pieces for ever, there is what is called the 50-move rule. If no piece has been taken and no Pawn move has been made in 50 moves, then a draw may again be claimed.

As you improve, you will come to recognise positions where there is really nothing either of you can do, and in that case you and your opponent can simply agree that the game is drawn. You are not likely to agree to a draw as quickly as one player did against a Czechoslovak grandmaster called Vlastimil Hort at Hastings recently. Hort arrived forty-five minutes late for a game and offered a draw after only three moves – because no one in his hotel had woken him up and he said he could not play chess before he had had breakfast!

In the same way as some positions are clearly drawn, so there are some positions that are equally clearly lost, and in that case, rather than wait to be checkmated, you are allowed to do what is called resigning. It is rather like a general surrendering before every soldier has been killed in a battle. He knows he has lost, so there is no point in going on. In fact, in

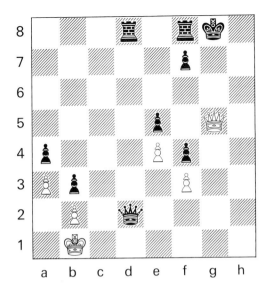

chess it is considered unsporting to continue when you know you have lost.

In the old days, when you threatened your opponent's King, you had to say 'check', but now you no longer have to do so. It can happen that you do not notice you are in check and you make a move leaving your King in check. Clearly you cannot do this, because if you did, your King would be taken next move and the game would be over. So you must take the move back and play again. If you can get out of check by moving the piece you moved wrongly, then you must. If you cannot, then you must play some other move with another piece that will get you out of check. This is the only time according to the rules in a game of chess that you are allowed to take a move back. Of course, if you make some frightful blunder, then your opponent might smile kindly and invite you to take it back and play another move. That would be sporting, but once you have made a move, you cannot take it back, or ask to take it back.

So that both players are quite clear about this, there is a very simple rule. If you touch a piece, you must move it. When you let go of the piece, the move is over. The only exception is if you want to adjust your pieces on their squares because they are untidy, in which case you must tell your opponent that that is what you are doing. This touching rule is very important and you should always play to it even in the friendliest of games because it will help you acquire a good habit – think before you move. Look all round the board, weigh up the various opportunities you have for attack or defence, and do not touch a piece until you have finally made up your mind about what you want to do. Dr Tarrasch had a rule for this: sit on your hands!

Once you have learned all the moves and the rules, you will probably start to play chess in a club, either at school or in your home town. And there you will come across a strange device called a chess clock. The object of this clock is to make you play reasonably quickly, not at breakneck speed, but at a sensible speed. In international chess they play forty moves in two and a half hours each, but you can arrange things just as you like.

You can have an hour for all your moves, or a quarter of an hour, or even five minutes.

A chess clock is actually two clocks, each with a little plunger on the top. The clocks are connected, so when you push down the plunger on your clock, your clock stops and your opponent's clock begins. At the beginning of the game you set the clocks to the amount of time you want to allow, say half an hour each. Five minutes before time is up, the minute hand begins to raise a little flag on the clockface. When your time is up, the flag drops and the game is over. If your flag drops first, you lose; it is called losing on time and it happens to the very best of players. It is not likely to happen to you until you become good, and you might play chess all your life without ever seeing a chess clock. But if you ever do, that is how it works!

Now that you are coming to the end of this book you will want to go on and read other chess books. We have used what is called the algebraic notation to describe games, but there are two other ways of writing down games which you should know. The first is the abbreviated algebraic. In this system, you simply give the square to which the piece is going, as you can see in the example below. The other system is called 'descriptive'. Each piece and each square has a name. All the pieces which start the game on the King's side are called King's pieces, and those on the Queen's side are called after the Queen. For example, the Rook on the Queen's side is called the Queen's Rook, the Knight is called the Queen's Knight, and so on. And exactly the same on the King's side. So, if you move the Queen's Pawn (that is, the Pawn in front of the Queen) forward two squares in the opening, you would write P–Q4: the Pawn has gone from the second square in the Queen's file to the fourth square.

In descriptive notation, White's moves are written down as they are seen from White's side of the board, and Black's moves from Black's side. So every square has two names, one for White and one for Black. For example e4 is White's K4 and Black's K5. Here is a little game given in all three notations, which will show how they all work:

| FULL ALGEBRAIC | | SHORT ALGEBRAIC | | DESCRIPTIVE | |
|---|---|---|---|---|---|
| 1 d2–d4 | Ng8–f6 | 1 d4 | Nf6 | 1 P–Q4 | N–KB3 |
| 2 c2–c4 | e7–e5 | 2 c4 | e5 | 2 P–QB4 | P–K4 |
| 3 d4xe5 | Nf6–g4 | 3 dxe5 | Ng4 | 3 PxP | N–N5 |
| 4 Ng1–f3 | Nb8–c6 | 4 Nf3 | Nc6 | 4 N–KB3 | N–QB3 |
| 5 Bc1–f4 | Bf8–b4+ | 5 Bf4 | Bb4+ | 5 B–B4 | B–N5ch |
| 6 Nb1–d2 | Qd8–e7 | 6 Nbd2 | Qe7 | 6 QN–Q2 | Q–K2 |
| 7 a2–a3 | Ng4xe5 | 7 a3 | Ngxe5 | 7 P–QR3 | KNxKP |
| 8 a3xb4 | Ne5–d3 mate | 8 axb4 | Nd3 mate | 8 PxB | N–Q6 mate |

*Notes:*

1 . . . *N–KB3*: The Knight moves to the third square on the King's Bishop's file, counting from Black's side, because it is a Black move.

3 *d4xe5*: In short, *dxe5*, or some people write even shorter just *de5*: or *de*. In descriptive, this becomes *PxP* (Pawn takes Pawn), you always write what is taken in this form, not the square it is taken on.

3 . . . *N–N5*: In fact this is *N–KN5*, but since no Knight can move to *QN5* there is no need to add the extra *K*.

5 . . . *B–N5ch*: Descriptive usually uses 'ch' for check.

6 *Nb1–d2*: Both White Knights can go to d2. In short algebraic we write 6 *Nbd2* or 6 *N1d2* to say that it is the Knight on the b-file or the first rank which moves. In descriptive it's *QN–Q2*, the Queen's Knight which makes the move, or we could write *N(N1)–Q2*.

7 . . . *KNxKP*: King's Knight takes King's Pawn. Both Knights can take this Pawn, so *NxKP* is not enough, and the KN can take three different Pawns, so *KNxP* is also not sufficient.

Like anything else, being good at chess is a matter of practice. But if you really want to be good, do not always practise against the same opponent. Try to find players slightly better than you; if they are too much better, you will not understand how they managed to beat you. If there is a school club, join it; failing that, join a local club. If you do not know of any clubs near you, write to: The British Chess Federation, 4 The Close, Norwich, Norfolk.

The Federation will also tell you where tournaments are being held. Go and watch really good players; watch the BBC TV programme 'The Mastergame', where you will see the finest players in the world.

Read books about the game. For instance: *Chess* by Edward Lasker; *Book of Chess Positions* by C.H. O'D. Alexander; *Learn Chess* (2 vols) by Alexander and Beach; *The Game of Chess* by H. Golombek; *Teach Yourself Chess* by Abrahams. And as you improve, read books by some of the really brilliant players like: *Masters of the Chess Board* by Richard Reti; *Larsen's Best Games* by Bent Larsen; *My System* by Nimzo-witsch; and *Sixty Memorable Games* by Fischer.

Even more important, play. Be pleased when you win, try to work out why you lost the odd games you are bound to lose, but if you want to enjoy the game more and play better, then quite simply, play chess.

# SIX: Answers to Puzzles

*(Page 16)*

PUZZLE 1

Black has not lost – yet. He has two squares where his King is safe – g7 or g8. White is going to win – and quickly, but to see just how, wait until the chapter on 'endgames'.

PUZZLE 2

It looks as if Black's Knight can either take the Rook on d8 or get in the way on b8. But look at that Bishop lurking on g2. If the Knight did move, then the King would be in check from that Bishop – so Black is checkmate.

PUZZLE 3

Black has nothing to do. He is in check from the Bishop on c3 and all his escape squares are covered by the White King or blocked by his own Pawn on h7. Which just goes to show that a King can give mate!

PUZZLE 4

White must have been pleased with Queen to h4. It looks like checkmate, but it is not. Black plays his Pawn from g7 to g5 which stops White's Queen check. But it also puts the White King in check from the Black Queen on h8. Can the King escape? He cannot; and it is White who is checkmate!

**The Rook** *(page 22)*

PUZZLE 1

White plays 1 *Rh2–e2+* winning the Rook on e8 by X-Ray attack. Notice that 1 *Rh2–h5+* is less good because Black can move his King to d4 or d6 and protect the X-Rayed Rook.

PUZZLE 2

1 *Rb3–b8* is not checkmate, because Black plays 1 . . . *Nc7–e8+*

in reply. But 1 *Rh4–h8* is indeed checkmate; White's own King prevents the Black King from escaping forwards.

PUZZLE 3

White can move the pinned Bishop! After 1 *Bd2–f4 +!* Black loses his Rook on d8. He must move his King out of check, then White plays *Rd1xd8*. This is an example of the Discovered Attack; the Bishop moves to uncover an attack by the Rook. Always remember that a piece is only completely pinned when it is pinned to the King; if it is pinned to Queen or Rook, it can still legally move away.

PUZZLE 4

Neither! After 1 . . . *Ke7xe6* comes the X-Ray attack, 2 *Rh3–h6 +*; while after 1 . . . *Qd6xe6* comes the pin, 2 *Rh3–e3*.

## The Knight (*page* 28)

PUZZLE 1

1 *Ng5–f7 +* forks King and Queen.

PUZZLE 2

White plays 1 *Rh1–h8 +!* and Black must take the Rook or his Queen is lost by X-Ray. And that leaves us in the position of Puzzle 1.

PUZZLE 3

The Pawn fork sets up the Knight fork! White plays 1 *f5–f6 +!* attacking both King and Queen. If Black takes with the Queen, then the Knight will fork on h5; or if Black takes with the King, then the fork comes on d5.

PUZZLE 4

White starts with 1 *Rc2–h2 +* when the Black King must go to g8. And then comes 2 *Nc6–e7* checkmate, a sort of semi-smothered mate. It's interesting that if you start with the Black

King already on g8 instead of h8, then White still mates in two moves: 1 Nc6–e7+ Kg8–h7 2 Rc2–h2 mate.

## The Bishop (page 34)

PUZZLE 1

It's the Pawn which does the work here: 1 e5–e6+ attacks both Queen and King, so it must be taken. But 1 . . . Qf7xe6 gets pinned by 2 Bf1–h3, or 1 . . . Kd7xe6 also loses the Queen after 2 Bf1–c4+.

PUZZLE 2

This is a funny sort of back rank mate with Rook and Bishop. White plays 1 Bh4–f6! and nothing can stop 2 Rh1–h8 from being checkmate.

PUZZLE 3

1 Bg5–f6+ forces the King where the Knight can finish him off: 1 . . . Kh8–g8 and now 2 Ng4–h6 is checkmate.

PUZZLE 4

Remember those smothered mates with the Knight? White here played 1 Ng5–e6! giving smothered mate not to the King but the Queen. The Knight can't be taken because the d7 Pawn is pinned.

## The Queen (page 40)

PUZZLE 1

1 Qg4–e6 is suddenly checkmate. The two Rooks stop Black's King from moving away sideways.

PUZZLE 2

White could un-pin the Bishop with 1 Bd3–e2 or 1 Bd3–c2, protecting his Queen, but he has far better. The discovered attack 1 Bd3–h7+! will win the Black Queen. Black must move out of check by taking the Bishop, then comes Qd1xd8.

PUZZLE 3

White wants his Queen on g7 or h8 where, protected by the Bishop on b2, she gives checkmate. So 1 *Qc2–c3!* is the right move. Black can do nothing against the threat of 2 *Qc3–h8* mate.

PUZZLE 4

No he can't! The tempting 1 *Qb2–g2+* is a horrible mistake; it allows the pin 1 . . . *Rc4–g4!* and it's White who loses his Queen!

**The King** (*page 46*)

PUZZLE 1

White must get rid of his Rook quickly! So he plays 1 *Rb1–b8+!* and whether Black takes it with King or with Bishop it will be stalemate.

PUZZLE 2

It's the same stalemate idea as the last position. White played 1 *Qf5–f2!* pinning the Black Queen to her King. Black must play 1 . . . *Qe3xf2* or he loses his Queen. And then it's stalemate!

PUZZLE 3

It looks hopeless for White, but he saves the game by another surprising stalemate. 1 *Kg8–h8!* is the right move; Black must then take the Pawn, or it will advance next move to become a Queen; but after 1 . . . *Ra7xg7* it's stalemate again.

PUZZLE 4

No stalemates this time – just careful King moves! 1 *Kg6–f6?* would be a bad mistake because after 1 . . . *Kc5–d5!* Black protects his Pawn, White must move his King away, and he loses his own Pawn. White must cleverly play instead 1 *Kg6–f7! Kc5–d5 2 Kf7–f6!* By losing a move, White reached this position with Black to play, and it's the Black King which must go away and lose the Pawn.

## The Pawn (*page 52*)

He was wrong. White played h5xg6 *en passant* and Black was checkmate from the Bishop!

1 c7–c8=Q is a big mistake because 1 . . . Rh1–h8 is then checkmate. White can save himself only with 1 c7–c8=N+! Black's King must move, and White escapes.

1 c5–c6! is the right move; after 1 . . . b7xc6, White plays 2 b5xa6! and his passed Pawn is too far away for Black to stop.

1 Kf1–g2! is the only good move. The careless 1 b6–b7 or 1 c6–c7 would lose to 1 . . . Kg4–f3! when nothing can stop 2 . . . g3–g2 checkmate!